THE POWER *of a* BLESSING

The

MESSAGE

THE READING BIBLE

WORDS TO SPEAK AND PRAY
FROM *The Message*

THE POWER *of a* BLESSING

EUGENE H. PETERSON

NAVPRESS

Bringing Truth to Life

COLORADO SPRINGS, COLORADO

ISBN 1-57683-521-9

THE MESSAGE Editorial Team: Terry Behimer, Stephen Board, Patricia Miller, Glynese Northam
THE POWER OF A BLESSING Editorial Team: Janel Breitenstein, Glynese Northam

Peterson, Eugene H., 1932-
  The power of a blessing : words to speak and pray from The Message /
Eugene H. Peterson.
    p. cm.
  ISBN 1-57683-521-9 (pbk.)
  1. Blessing and cursing in the Bible. 2. Bible--Quotations. I.
Title.
  BS680.B5P48 2004
  220.5′209--dc22

                        2003019721

Published in association with the literary agency of Alive Communications, Inc., 7680 Goddard St., Suite 200, Colorado Springs, CO 80920.

1 2 3 4 5 6 7 8 9 10 11 12 13 14 15 16 17 / 10 09 08 07 06 05 04

Printed in Canada

TABLE *of* CONTENTS

Tab. 242.

Kalmia latifolia
Die breitblättrige Kalmie

All these blessings will come down on you

and spread out beyond you because you have

responded to the Voice of GOD, your God.

—DEUTERONOMY 28:2

EXPERIENCE THE POWER
of a BLESSING

❦

A blessing is powerful. Blessings offer us comfort, protection, hope, vision — and even more: They represent God's best for us as his people. In a blessing, we are drawn into his plan and passion for our future.

Whether God blesses us or we bless one another, the power of a blessing lies in the One who truly gives the blessing: *God*. A blessing would be nearly fruitless if it relied merely on the power of the spoken word or the earnestness of the heart to move it from desire to reality, as if it were an incantation or a spell. The blessings that we speak can in fact bless other people because God allows them to bless other people. He actively "agrees" with us as we affirm his promises.

In that way, our relationship to him also has great power. God agrees with us and carries out our requests in part because of our position — of both blesser and blessed — as his children, whom he loves deeply. When God, or someone who speaks God's words, offers a blessing, it is almost as if the blesser is saying, "May you, as one who belongs to God, experience this: God's best."

A blessing is powerful because it aligns with God's will. First John 5 reminds us of "how bold and free we then become in his presence, freely asking according to his will, sure that he's listening. And if we're confident that he's listening, we know that what we've asked for is as good as ours" (vv. 14-15). Several times throughout Scripture, God willingly delivers blessings to his people, blessings that accomplish great things in the lives of his people:

> *"Listen to me, all you who are serious about right living*
> *and committed to seeking* GOD.
> *Ponder the rock from which you were cut,*
> *the quarry from which you were dug.*
> *Yes, ponder Abraham, your father,*
> *and Sarah, who bore you.*
> *Think of it! One solitary man when I called him,*
> *but once I blessed him, he multiplied." (Isaiah 51:1-2)*

God's blessing to Abraham began a covenant and a nation; his blessing of Mary foretold a Savior. A blessing relies on the character of God — his faithfulness, his wisdom, his goodness — and his long-ing to give us the best that he has for us.

If the power of a blessing lies in God's willingness, then the oppo-site is also true. A blessing cannot have true power unless it comes from God's hand. We see this in Numbers 23, when Balaak asks Balaam to curse Israel, and Balaam cannot: "Don't I have to be care-ful to say what GOD gives me to say?" We see it when Isaac unknow-ingly pronounces the blessing of the firstborn upon the younger Jacob, the chosen bearer of God's covenant to Israel, and has little blessing left for Esau. Yet this principle gives us much to be thankful for — "Nothing and no one can upset your plans" (Job 42:2). The power of a blessing lies within the loving will of our all-knowing God.

Blessings allow us the opportunity to take hold of God's willing-ness. They help us to participate with God in the best he has for us, moving closer to his greatest desires for us — even when those desires simply involve obedience on our part:

> "Go in peace. And may the God of Israel give you what you have asked of him." (1 Samuel 1:17)

> "Be bold and diligent. And GOD be with you as you do your best." (2 Chronicles 19:11)

"You're blessed when you've worked up a good appetite for God. He's food and drink in the best meal you'll ever eat." (Matthew 5:6)

Consistent with his character, God allows us to participate in his great plan as we bless one another. As Paul commends the Philippians, "Be energetic in your life of salvation, reverent and sensitive before God. That energy is *God's* energy, an energy deep within you, God himself willing and working at what will give him the most pleasure" (2:12-13). Even as we focus on God's actions and his power in fulfilling a blessing, we see ourselves pursuing the best, responding and obeying as God blesses us.

You're blessed when you meet Lady Wisdom . . . She's worth far more than money in the bank. (Proverbs 3:13)

May the Master of Peace himself give you the gift of getting along with each other at all times, in all ways. May the Master be truly among you! (2 Thessalonians 3:16)

When God blesses us, as he moves us more into his will, our identity is redefined. We become more like him, more like the people he longs for us to be. And in that way, a blessing is nearly a biblical naming ceremony, calling us out of our present selves to lay hold of his bigger plan — as when God blesses Jacob and renames him Israel (Genesis 32:22-32), or when Jesus blesses Simon and foretells of the church, now naming him Peter (Matthew 16:13-20). God blesses us and affirms our relationship with him, redefining us and making us more like him, taking us even further into his great story.

Because of this relationship and the larger context of time and place in which each blessing from Scripture occurs, use the references provided to look more deeply into the story in which each blessing comes about. Explore the surrounding passage from which each verse is taken. Meditate on their meanings, on their Source. And pray these words. Speak them over those you love, even over your enemies (Matthew 5:44). Encounter God and what he wants for us — and experience the power of a blessing.

Real help comes from GOD.
Your blessing clothes your people!

— *Psalm 3:8*

— THE MESSAGE *Team*

Open your mouth and taste,

open your eyes and see — how good GOD is.

Blessed are you who run to him.

—PSALM 34:8

BLESSINGS *for* GOD'S PEOPLE

Genesis 12:2-3, *from God to Abram*

> "I'll make you a great nation
>   and bless you.
> I'll make you famous;
>   you'll be a blessing.
> I'll bless those who bless you;
>   those who curse you I'll curse.
> All the families of the Earth
>   will be blessed through you."

Genesis 26:24, *from God to Isaac*

> I am the God of Abraham your father;
>   don't fear a thing because I'm with you.
> I'll bless you and make your children flourish
>   because of Abraham my servant.

Numbers 6:22-27, *from God to the people of Israel*

> GOD spoke to Moses: "Tell Aaron and his sons, This is how
> you are to bless the People of Israel. Say to them,
>
> GOD bless you and keep you,
> GOD smile on you and gift you,
> GOD look you full in the face
>   and make you prosper.
>
> In so doing, they will place my name on the People of Israel —
>   I will confirm it by blessing them."

Numbers 10:36, *Moses' request to God*

> Rest with us, GOD,
> Stay with the many,
> Many thousands of Israel.

Numbers 14:17-19, *Moses' request to God*

> "Now, please, let the power of the Master expand, enlarge
> itself greatly, along the lines you have laid out earlier when
> you said,

GOD, slow to get angry and huge in loyal love,

> forgiving iniquity and rebellion and sin;

Still, never just whitewashing sin.

> But extending the fallout of parents' sins

to children into the third,

> even the fourth generation.

> "Please forgive the wrongdoing of this people out of the extravagance of your loyal love just as all along, from the time they left Egypt, you have been forgiving this people."

Numbers 23:8-10, *from God to Israel, through Balaam*

How can I curse whom God has not cursed?

> How can I damn whom GOD has not damned?

From rock pinnacles I see them,

> from hilltops I survey them:

Look! a people camping off by themselves,

> thinking themselves outsiders among nations.

But who could ever count the dust of Jacob

> or take a census of cloud-of-dust Israel?

I want to die like these right-living people!

> I want an end just like theirs!

Numbers 23:19-24, *from God to Israel, through Balaam*

> God is not man, one given to lies,
>> and not a son of man changing his mind.
> Does he speak and not do what he says?
>> Does he promise and not come through?
> I was brought here to bless;
>> and now he's blessed — how can I change that?
> He has no bone to pick with Jacob,
>> he sees nothing wrong with Israel.
> GOD is with them,
>> and they're with him, shouting praises to their King.
> God brought them out of Egypt,
>> rampaging like a wild ox.
> No magic spells can bind Jacob,
>> no incantations can hold back Israel.
> People will look at Jacob and Israel and say,
>> "What a great thing has God done!"
> Look, a people rising to its feet, stretching like a lion,
>> a king-of-the-beasts, aroused,
> Unsleeping, unresting until its hunt is over
>> and it's eaten and drunk its fill.

Numbers 24:5-9, *from God to Israel, through Balaam*

Decree of Balaam son of Beor,
    yes, decree of a man with 20/20 vision;
Decree of a man who hears God speak,
    who sees what The Strong God shows him,
Who falls on his face in worship,
    who sees what's really going on.

What beautiful tents, Jacob,
    oh, your homes, Israel!
Like valleys stretching out in the distance,
    like gardens planted by rivers,
Like sweet herbs planted by the gardener GOD,
    like red cedars by pools and springs,
Their buckets will brim with water,
    their seed will spread life everywhere.
Their king will tower over Agag and his ilk,
    their kingdom surpassingly majestic.
God brought them out of Egypt,
    rampaging like a wild ox,
Gulping enemies like morsels of meat,
    crushing their bones, snapping their arrows.

Israel crouches like a lion and naps,

king-of-the-beasts — who dares disturb him?

Whoever blesses you is blessed,

whoever curses you is cursed.

Deuteronomy 1:10-11, *from Moses to the people of Israel*

"GOD, your God, has multiplied your numbers. Why, look at you — you rival the stars in the sky! And may GOD, the God-of-Your-Fathers, keep it up and multiply you another thousand times, bless you just as he promised."

Deuteronomy 26:15, *from the people of Israel to God*

Look down from your holy house in Heaven!

Bless your people Israel and the ground you gave us,

just as you promised our ancestors you would,

this land flowing with milk and honey.

Deuteronomy 28:1-14, *from Moses to the people of Israel*

If you listen obediently to the Voice of GOD, your God, and heartily obey all his commandments that I command you today, GOD, your God, will place you on high, high above all

the nations of the world. All these blessings will come down
on you and spread out beyond you because you have
responded to the Voice of GOD, your God:

> GOD's blessing inside the city,
> GOD's blessing in the country;
> GOD's blessing on your children,
>> the crops of your land,
>> the young of your livestock,
>> the calves of your herds,
>> the lambs of your flocks.
> GOD's blessing on your basket and bread bowl;
> GOD's blessing in your coming in,
> GOD's blessing in your going out.

GOD will defeat your enemies who attack you. They'll
come at you on one road and run away on seven roads.

GOD will order a blessing on your barns and workplaces;
he'll bless you in the land that GOD, your God, is giving you.

GOD will form you as a people holy to him, just as he
promised you, if you keep the commandments of GOD,
your God, and live the way he has shown you.

All the peoples on Earth will see you living under the Name
of GOD and hold you in respectful awe.

GOD will lavish you with good things: children from your womb, offspring from your animals, and crops from your land, the land that GOD promised your ancestors that he would give you. GOD will throw open the doors of his sky vaults and pour rain on your land on schedule and bless the work you take in hand. You will lend to many nations but you yourself won't have to take out a loan. GOD will make you the head, not the tail; you'll always be the top dog, never the bottom dog, as you obediently listen to and diligently keep the commands of GOD, your God, that I am commanding you today. Don't swerve an inch to the right or left from the words that I command you today by going off following and worshiping other gods.

Deuteronomy 33:1-5,26-29, *from Moses, man of God, to the people of Israel before his death*

GOD came down from Sinai,
     he dawned from Seir upon them;
He radiated light from Mount Paran,
     coming with ten thousand holy angels
And tongues of fire
     streaming from his right hand.

Oh, how you love the people,
> all his holy ones are palmed in your left hand.

They sit at your feet,
> honoring your teaching,

The Revelation commanded by Moses,
> as the assembly of Jacob's inheritance.

Thus GOD became king in Jeshurun
> as the leaders and tribes of Israel gathered. . . .

There is none like God, Jeshurun,
> riding to your rescue through the skies,
> his dignity haloed by clouds.

The ancient God is home
> on a foundation of everlasting arms.

He drove out the enemy before you
> and commanded, "Destroy!"

Israel lived securely,
> the fountain of Jacob undisturbed

In grain and wine country
> and, oh yes, his heavens drip dew.

Lucky Israel! Who has it as good as you?
> A people *saved* by GOD!

The Shield who defends you,
>the Sword who brings triumph.
Your enemies will come crawling on their bellies
>and you'll march on their backs.

2 Samuel 15:20, *from David to Ittai the Gittite*

"God's grace and truth go with you!"

2 Chronicles 19:11, *from King Jehoshapat to the appointed Levites, priests, and family heads*

"Be bold and diligent. And GOD be with you as you do your best."

2 Chronicles 30:18-19, *Hezekiah's request to God*

"May GOD who is all good, pardon and forgive everyone who sincerely desires GOD, the God of our ancestors."

Psalm 3:8

Real help comes from GOD.
Your blessing clothes your people!

Psalm 28:9, *from David to God*

>Save your people
>>and bless your heritage.
>Care for them;
>>carry them like a good shepherd.

Psalm 31:19-20, *from David to God*

>What a stack of blessing you have piled up
>>for those who worship you,
>Ready and waiting for all who run to you
>>to escape an unkind world.
>You hide them safely away
>>from the opposition.

Psalm 33:12

>Blessed is the country with GOD for God;
>>blessed are the people he's put in his will.

Psalm 34:8

>Open your mouth and taste, open your eyes and see —
>>how good GOD is.
>Blessed are you who run to him.

Psalm 40:4

> Blessed are you who give yourselves over to GOD,
>> turn your backs on the world's "sure thing,"
>> ignore what the world worships.

Psalm 65:4

> Blessed are the chosen! Blessed the guest
>> at home in your place!
> We expect our fill of good things
>> in your house, your heavenly manse.

Psalm 67:1

> God, mark us with grace
>> and blessing! Smile!

Psalm 84:3-7, *from Korah to God*

> Birds find nooks and crannies in your house,
>> sparrows and swallows make nests there.
> They lay their eggs and raise their young,
>> singing their songs in the place where we worship.

GOD of the Angel Armies! King! God!
　　How blessed they are to live and sing there!

And how blessed all those in whom you live,
　　whose lives become roads you travel;
They wind through lonesome valleys, come upon brooks,
　　discover cool springs and pools brimming with rain!
God-traveled, these roads curve up the mountain, and
　　at the last turn — Zion! God in full view!

Psalm 90:12-17, *from Moses to God*

Oh! Teach us to live well!
　　Teach us to live wisely and well!
Come back, GOD — how long do we have to wait? —
　　and treat your servants with kindness for a change.
Surprise us with love at daybreak;
　　then we'll skip and dance all the day long.
Make up for the bad times with some good times;
　　we've seen enough evil to last a lifetime.
Let your servants see what you're best at —
　　the ways you rule and bless your children.

And let the loveliness of our Lord, our God, rest on us,
confirming the work that we do.
Oh, yes. Affirm the work that we do!

Psalm 112:1-9

Hallelujah!
Blessed man, blessed woman, who fear GOD,
Who cherish and relish his commandments,
Their children robust on the earth,
And the homes of the upright — how blessed!
Their houses brim with wealth
And a generosity that never runs dry.
Sunrise breaks through the darkness for good people —
God's grace and mercy and justice!
The good person is generous and lends lavishly;
No shuffling or stumbling around for this one,
But a sterling and solid and lasting reputation.
Unfazed by rumor and gossip,
Heart ready, trusting in GOD,
Spirit firm, unperturbed,
Ever blessed, relaxed among enemies,
They lavish gifts on the poor —

A generosity that goes on, and on, and on.
An honored life! A beautiful life!

Psalm 115:12-18

O GOD, remember us and bless us,
  bless the families of Israel and Aaron.
And let GOD bless all who fear GOD —
  bless the small, bless the great.
Oh, let GOD enlarge your families —
  giving growth to you, growth to your children.
May you be blessed by GOD,
  by GOD, who made heaven and earth.
The heaven of heavens is for GOD,
  but he put us in charge of the earth.

Dead people can't praise GOD —
  not a word to be heard from those buried in the ground.
But we bless GOD, oh yes —
  we bless him now, we bless him always!
Hallelujah!

Psalm 118:26

> Blessed are you who enter in GOD's name —
>> from GOD's house we bless you!

Psalm 128, *a pilgrim song*

> All you who fear GOD, how blessed you are!
>> how happily you walk on his smooth straight road!
> You worked hard and deserve all you've got coming.
>> Enjoy the blessing! Revel in the goodness!
>
> Your wife will bear children as a vine bears grapes,
>> your household lush as a vineyard,
> The children around your table
>> as fresh and promising as young olive shoots.
> Stand in awe of God's Yes.
>> Oh, how he blesses the one who fears GOD!
>
> Enjoy the good life in Jerusalem
>> every day of your life.
> And enjoy your grandchildren.
>> Peace to Israel!

Psalm 133, *from David*

> How wonderful, how beautiful,
>> when brothers and sisters get along!
> It's like costly anointing oil
>> flowing down head and beard,
> Flowing down Aaron's beard,
>> flowing down the collar of his priestly robes.
> It's like the dew on Mount Hermon
>> flowing down the slopes of Zion.
> Yes, that's where GOD commands the blessing,
>> ordains eternal life.

Isaiah 44:1-5, *from God to Israel*

> "But for now, dear servant Jacob, listen —
>> yes, you, Israel, my personal choice.
> GOD who made you has something to say to you;
>> the God who formed you in the womb wants to
>> help you.
> Don't be afraid, dear servant Jacob,
>> Jeshurun, the one I chose.
> For I will pour water on the thirsty ground
>> and send streams coursing through the parched earth.

I will pour my Spirit into your descendants
    and my blessing on your children.
They shall sprout like grass on the prairie,
    like willows alongside creeks.
This one will say, 'I am GOD's,'
    and another will go by the name Jacob;
That one will write on his hand 'GOD's property' —
    and be proud to be called Israel."

Jeremiah 17:7-8

"But blessed is the man who trusts me, GOD,
    the woman who sticks with GOD.
They're like trees replanted in Eden,
    putting down roots near the rivers —
Never a worry through the hottest of summers,
    never dropping a leaf,
Serene and calm through droughts,
    bearing fresh fruit every season."

Ezekiel 34:25-31, *from God concerning his people Israel*

"'I'll make a covenant of peace with them. I'll banish fierce
animals from the country so the sheep can live safely in the

wilderness and sleep in the forest. I'll make them and everything around my hill a blessing. I'll send down plenty of rain in season — showers of blessing! The trees in the orchards will bear fruit, the ground will produce, they'll feel content and safe on their land, and they'll realize that I am GOD when I break them out of their slavery and rescue them from their slave masters.

"'No longer will they be exploited by outsiders and ravaged by fierce beasts. They'll live safe and sound, fearless and free. I'll give them rich gardens, lavish in vegetables — no more living half-starved, no longer taunted by outsiders.

"'They'll know, beyond doubting, that I, GOD, am their God, that I'm with them and that they, the people Israel, are my people. Decree of GOD, the Master:

You are my dear flock,
the flock of my pasture, my human flock,
And I am your God.
Decree of GOD, the Master.'"

Luke 1:45, *from Elizabeth to her cousin Mary*

Blessed woman, who believed what God said,
believed every word would come true!

Luke 6:20-23, *from Jesus to his disciples and the gathered congregation*

> "You're blessed when you've lost it all.
> God's kingdom is there for the finding.

> "You're blessed when you're ravenously hungry.
> Then you're ready for the Messianic meal.

> "You're blessed when the tears flow freely.
> Joy comes with the morning.

> "Count yourself blessed every time someone cuts you
> down or throws you out, every time someone smears or
> blackens your name to discredit me. What it means is that
> the truth is too close for comfort and that that person is
> uncomfortable. You can be glad when that happens — skip
> like a lamb, if you like! — for even though they don't like it,
> I do . . . and all heaven applauds. And know that you are in
> good company; my preachers and witnesses have always
> been treated like this."

Luke 8:48, *from Jesus to the woman healed of her hemorrhaging*

> "You took a risk trusting me, and now you're healed and
> whole. Live well, live blessed!"

Luke 11:28, *from Jesus to a woman in the crowd*

"Blessed are those who hear God's Word and guard it with their lives!"

Luke 12:37-38, *from Jesus*

"Lucky the servants whom the master finds on watch! He'll put on an apron, sit them at the table, and serve them a meal, sharing his wedding feast with them. It doesn't matter what time of the night he arrives; they're awake — and so blessed!"

John 17:15-26, *from Jesus to God*

I'm not asking that you take them out of the world
But that you guard them from the Evil One.
They are no more defined by the world
Than I am defined by the world.
Make them holy — consecrated — with the truth;
Your word is consecrating truth.
In the same way that you gave me a mission in the world,
I give them a mission in the world.
I'm consecrating myself for their sakes
So they'll be truth-consecrated in their mission.

I'm praying not only for them
But also for those who will believe in me
Because of them and their witness about me.
The goal is for all of them to become one heart and mind —
Just as you, Father, are in me and I in you,
So they might be one heart and mind with us.
Then the world might believe that you, in fact, sent me.
The same glory you gave me, I gave them,
So they'll be as unified and together as we are —
I in them and you in me.
Then they'll be mature in this oneness,
And give the godless world evidence
That you've sent me and loved them
In the same way you've loved me.

Father, I want those you gave me
To be with me, right where I am,
So they can see my glory, the splendor you gave me,
Having loved me
Long before there ever was a world.
Righteous Father, the world has never known you,
But I have known you, and these disciples know
That you sent me on this mission.

I have made your very being known to them —
Who you are and what you do —
And continue to make it known,
So that your love for me
Might be in them
Exactly as I am in them.

Romans 15:5, *from Paul to all of the Christians in Rome*

May our dependably steady and warmly personal God develop maturity in you so that you get along with each other as well as Jesus gets along with us all.

Romans 15:13, *from Paul to all of the Christians in Rome*

Oh! May the God of green hope fill you up with joy, fill you up with peace, so that your believing lives, filled with the life-giving energy of the Holy Spirit, will brim over with hope!

Romans 15:33, *from Paul to all of the Christians in Rome*

God's peace be with all of you. Oh, yes!

I Corinthians 1:3-6, *from Paul, along with his friend Sosthenes, to God's church at Corinth*

> May all the gifts and benefits that come from God our Father, and the Master, Jesus Christ, be yours.
>
> Every time I think of you — and I think of you often! — I thank God for your lives of free and open access to God, given by Jesus. There's no end to what has happened in you — it's beyond speech, beyond knowledge. The evidence of Christ has been clearly verified in your lives.

2 Corinthians 13:14, *from Paul and Timothy to God's congregation in Corinth, and to believers all over Achaia province*

> The amazing grace of the Master, Jesus Christ, the extravagant love of God, the intimate friendship of the Holy Spirit, be with all of you.

Galatians 6:18, *from Paul and his companions in faith to the Galatian churches*

> May what our Master Jesus Christ gives freely be deeply and personally yours, my friends. Oh, yes!

Ephesians 1:17-21, *from Paul to the faithful Christians in Ephesus*

I ask — ask the God of our Master, Jesus Christ, the God of glory — to make you intelligent and discerning in knowing him personally, your eyes focused and clear, so that you can see exactly what it is he is calling you to do, grasp the immensity of this glorious way of life he has for Christians, oh, the utter extravagance of his work in us who trust him — endless energy, boundless strength!

All this energy issues from Christ: God raised him from death and set him on a throne in deep heaven, in charge of running the universe, everything from galaxies to governments, no name and no power exempt from his rule. And not just for the time being, but *forever*.

Ephesians 3:16-19, *from Paul to the faithful Christians in Ephesus*

I ask him to strengthen you by his Spirit — not a brute strength but a glorious inner strength — that Christ will live in you as you open the door and invite him in. And I ask him that with both feet planted firmly on love, you'll be able to take in with all Christians the extravagant dimensions of Christ's love. Reach out and experience the breadth! Test its length! Plumb the depths! Rise to the heights! Live full lives, full in the fullness of God.

Ephesians 6:23-24, *from Paul to the faithful Christians in Ephesus*

Love mixed with faith be yours from God the Father and from the Master, Jesus Christ. Pure grace and nothing but grace be with all who love our Master, Jesus Christ.

Philippians 4:1, *from Paul and Timothy to all the Christians at Philippi*

My dear, dear friends! I love you so much. I do want the very best for you. You make me feel such joy, fill me with such pride. Don't waver. Stay on track, steady in God.

2 Thessalonians 3:16,18, *from Paul, together with Silas and Timothy, to the church of the Thessalonian Christians*

May the Master of Peace himself give you the gift of getting along with each other at all times, in all ways. May the Master be truly among you! . . .

The incredible grace of our Master, Jesus Christ, be with all of you!

2 Timothy 1:18, *from Paul to Timothy*

> May God on the Last Day treat him [Onesiphorus] as well
> as he treated me.

2 Timothy 4:22, *from Paul to Timothy*

> God be with you. Grace be with you.

Philemon 4-7, *from Paul, with his brother Timothy, to Philemon*

> Every time your name comes up in my prayers, I say, "Oh,
> thank you, God!" I keep hearing of the love and faith you
> have for the Master Jesus, which brims over to other
> Christians. And I keep praying that this faith we hold in
> common keeps showing up in the good things we do, and
> that people recognize Christ in all of it. Friend, you have no
> idea how good your love makes me feel, doubly so when I
> see your hospitality to fellow believers.

Hebrews 13:20-21, *from the author of Hebrews to Jewish believers*

> May God, who puts all things together,
>   makes all things whole,

Who made a lasting mark through the sacrifice of Jesus,
　　　the sacrifice of blood that sealed the eternal covenant,
Who led Jesus, our Great Shepherd,
　　　up and alive from the dead,
Now put you together, provide you
　　　with everything you need to please him,
Make us into what gives him most pleasure,
　　　by means of the sacrifice of Jesus, the Messiah.
All glory to Jesus forever and always!
　　　Oh, yes, yes, yes.

1 Peter 1:2, *from Peter to the scattered exiles*

God the Father has his eye on each of you, and has deter-
mined by the work of the Spirit to keep you obedient
through the sacrifice of Jesus. May everything good from
God be yours!

Revelation 1:3, *from the apostle John*

How blessed the reader! How blessed the hearers and keepers
of these oracle words, all the words written in this book!
　　　Time is just about up.

Revelation 14:13, *from the apostle John*

> I heard a voice out of Heaven, "Write this: Blessed are those who die in the Master from now on; how blessed to die that way!"
>
> "Yes," says the Spirit, "and blessed rest from their hard, hard work. None of what they've done is wasted; God blesses them for it all in the end."

Revelation 20:5-6, *from the apostle John*

> The rest of the dead did not live until the thousand years were up. This is the first resurrection — and those involved most blessed, most holy. No second death for them! They're priests of God and Christ; they'll reign with him a thousand years.

Revelation 22:7, *from the Angel to the apostle John*

> "And tell them, 'Yes, I'm on my way!' Blessed be the one who keeps the words of the prophecy of this book."

Revelation 22:14, *from Jesus*

> "How blessed are those who wash their robes! The Tree of
> Life is theirs for good, and they'll walk through the gates to
> the City."

GOD bless you and keep you,

GOD smile on you and gift you,

GOD look you full in the face

and make you prosper.

— Numbers 6:24-26

You're blessed when you stay on course,

walking steadily on the road revealed by GOD.

You're blessed when you follow his directions,

doing your best to find him.

— PSALM 119:1-2

Blessings *for* Character

Deuteronomy 30:16, *from Moses to the people of Israel*

> Love GOD, your God. Walk in his ways. Keep his com-
> mandments, regulations, and rules so that you will live,
> really live, live exuberantly, blessed by GOD, your God, in
> the land you are about to enter and possess.

1 Chronicles 22:12-13, *from King David to his son, Solomon*

> And may GOD also give you discernment and understanding
> when he puts you in charge of Israel so that you will rule in
> reverent obedience under GOD's Revelation. That's what
> will make you successful, following the directions and doing
> the things that GOD commanded Moses for Israel.
> Courage! Take charge! Don't be timid; don't hold back.

Psalm 111:10

> The good life begins in the fear of GOD —
> Do that and you'll know the blessing of GOD.
> His Hallelujah lasts forever!

Psalm 119:1-2

> You're blessed when you stay on course,
> walking steadily on the road revealed by GOD.
> You're blessed when you follow his directions,
> doing your best to find him.

Psalm 141:5

> May the Just One set me straight,
> may the Kind One correct me,
> Don't let sin anoint my head.
> I'm praying hard against their evil ways!

Proverbs 3:13-18

> You're blessed when you meet Lady Wisdom,
> when you make friends with Madame Insight.

She's worth far more than money in the bank;
> her friendship is better than a big salary.
Her value exceeds all the trappings of wealth;
> nothing you could wish for holds a candle to her.
With one hand she gives long life,
> with the other she confers recognition.
Her manner is beautiful,
> her life wonderfully complete.
She's the very Tree of Life to those who embrace her.
> Hold her tight — and be blessed!

Proverbs 3:33

GOD's curse blights the house of the wicked,
> but he blesses the home of the righteous.

Proverbs 8:32-35, *from Lady Wisdom*

"So, my dear friends, listen carefully;
> those who embrace these my ways are most blessed.
Mark a life of discipline and live wisely;
> don't squander your precious life.

Blessed the man, blessed the woman, who listens to me,
    awake and ready for me each morning,
    alert and responsive as I start my day's work.
When you find me, you find life, real life,
    to say nothing of GOD's good pleasure."

Proverbs 10:6-7

Blessings accrue on a good and honest life. . . .
A good and honest life is a blessed memorial.

Proverbs 11:25-26

The one who blesses others is abundantly blessed;
    those who help others are helped.

Curses on those who drive a hard bargain!
    Blessings on all who play fair and square!

Proverbs 14:21

It's criminal to ignore a neighbor in need,
    but compassion for the poor — what a blessing!

Proverbs 16:20

> It pays to take life seriously;
>> things work out when you trust in GOD.

Proverbs 22:9

> Generous hands are blessed hands
>> because they give bread to the poor.

Proverbs 28:14

> A tenderhearted person lives a blessed life.

Proverbs 29:18

> If people can't see what God is doing,
>> they stumble all over themselves;
> But when they attend to what he reveals,
>> they are most blessed.

Proverbs 31:29, *to the good woman from her children and husband*

> "Many women have done wonderful things,
>> but you've outclassed them all!"

Isaiah 56:1-2

> GOD's Message:
> "Guard my common good:
>> Do what's right and do it in the right way,
> For salvation is just around the corner,
>> my setting-things-right is about to go into action.
> How blessed are you who enter into these things,
>> you men and women who embrace them,
> Who keep Sabbath and don't defile it,
>> who watch your step and don't do anything evil!"

Matthew 5:3-12, *from Jesus to his climbing companions*

> "You're blessed when you're at the end of your rope. With less of you there is more of God and his rule.
>
> "You're blessed when you feel you've lost what is most dear to you. Only then can you be embraced by the One most dear to you.
>
> "You're blessed when you're content with just who you are — no more, no less. That's the moment you find yourselves proud owners of everything that can't be bought.

"You're blessed when you've worked up a good appetite for God. He's food and drink in the best meal you'll ever eat.

"You're blessed when you care. At the moment of being 'care-full,' you find yourselves cared for.

"You're blessed when you get your inside world — your mind and heart — put right. Then you can see God in the outside world.

"You're blessed when you can show people how to cooperate instead of compete or fight. That's when you discover who you really are, and your place in God's family.

"You're blessed when your commitment to God provokes persecution. The persecution drives you even deeper into God's kingdom.

"Not only that — count yourselves blessed every time people put you down or throw you out or speak lies about you to discredit me. What it means is that the truth is too close for comfort and they are uncomfortable. You can be glad when that happens — give a cheer, even! — for though they don't like it, *I* do! And all heaven applauds. And know that you are in good company. My prophets and witnesses have always gotten into this kind of trouble."

Luke 1:28, *from Gabriel to Mary*

> Good morning!
> You're beautiful with God's beauty,
> Beautiful inside and out!
> God be with you.

John 13:15,17, *from Jesus to his disciples*

> "I've laid down a pattern for you. . . . If you understand
> what I'm telling you, act like it — and live a blessed life."

Acts 4:29-30, *from friends of Peter and John to God, after the apostles' release from prison*

> "Give your servants fearless confidence in preaching your
> Message, as you stretch out your hand to us in healings and
> miracles and wonders done in the name of your holy ser-
> vant Jesus."

Acts 20:35, *from Paul to the leaders of the Ephesian congregation*

> "In everything I've done, I have demonstrated to you how
> necessary it is to work on behalf of the weak and not exploit

them. You'll not likely go wrong here if you keep remembering that our Master said, 'You're far happier giving than getting.'"

1 Corinthians 16:13-14, *from Paul, along with his friend Sosthenes, to God's church at Corinth*

Keep your eyes open, hold tight to your convictions, give it all you've got, be resolute, and love without stopping.

2 Corinthians 13:11, *from Paul and Timothy to God's congregation in Corinth, and to believers all over Achaia province*

Be cheerful. Keep things in good repair. Keep your spirits up. Think in harmony. Be agreeable. Do all that, and the God of love and peace will be with you for sure.

Colossians 1:9-14, *from Paul, together with Timothy, to the Colossians*

Be assured that from the first day we heard of you, we haven't stopped praying for you, asking God to give you wise minds and spirits attuned to his will, and so acquire a thorough understanding of the ways in which God works. We pray that you'll live well for the Master, making him proud of you as you work hard in his orchard. As you learn more and more how God works, you will learn how to do *your* work. We pray that you'll have the strength to stick it out over the long haul — not the grim strength of gritting your teeth but the glory-strength God gives. It is strength that endures the unendurable and spills over into joy, thanking the Father who makes us strong enough to take part in everything bright and beautiful that he has for us.

Colossians 2:2, *from Paul, together with Timothy, to the Colossians*

I want you woven into a tapestry of love, in touch with everything there is to know of God. Then you will have minds confident and at rest, focused on Christ, God's great mystery.

Colossians 2:6-8, *from Paul, together with Timothy, to the Colossians*

My counsel for you is simple and straightforward: Just go ahead with what you've been given. You received Christ Jesus, the Master; now *live* him. You're deeply rooted in him. You're well constructed upon him. You know your way around the faith. Now do what you've been taught. School's out; quit studying the subject and start *living* it! And let your living spill over into thanksgiving.

1 Thessalonians 3:12, *from Paul, together with Silas and Timothy, to the church at Thessalonica*

And may the Master pour on the love so it fills your lives and splashes over on everyone around you, just as it does from us to you. May you be infused with strength and purity, filled with confidence in the presence of God our Father when our Master Jesus arrives with all his followers.

May the Master take you by the hand

and lead you along the path

of God's love and Christ's endurance.

— 2 Thessalonians 3:5

BLESSINGS *for* TIMES
OF TROUBLE

❧

Job 1:21, *from Job to God*

> Naked I came from my mother's womb,
> > naked I'll return to the womb of the earth.
> GOD gives, GOD takes.
> > God's name be ever blessed.

Psalm 20:1-5, *from David*

> GOD answer you on the day you crash,
> The name God-of-Jacob put you out of harm's reach,
> Send reinforcements from Holy Hill,
> Dispatch from Zion fresh supplies,
> Exclaim over your offerings,
> Celebrate your sacrifices,

Give you what your heart desires,
Accomplish your plans.

When you win, we plan to raise the roof
    and lead the parade with our banners.
May all your wishes come true!

Psalm 94:12-15

How blessed the man you train, GOD,
    the woman you instruct in your Word,
Providing a circle of quiet within the clamor of evil,
    while a jail is being built for the wicked.
GOD will never walk away from his people,
    never desert his precious people.
Rest assured that justice is on its way
    and every good heart put right.

Psalm 146:1-5

Hallelujah!
    O my soul, praise GOD!
All my life long I'll praise GOD,
    singing songs to my God as long as I live.

Don't put your life in the hands of experts
    who know nothing of life, of *salvation* life.
Mere humans don't have what it takes;
    when they die, their projects die with them.
Instead, get help from the God of Jacob,
    put your hope in GOD and know real blessing!

1 Corinthians 1:9, *from Paul, along with his friend Sosthenes, to God's church
at Corinth*

God, who got you started in this spiritual adventure, shares
with us the life of his Son and our Master Jesus. He will
never give up on you. Never forget that.

2 Corinthians 1:3-5, *from Paul and Timothy to God's congregation in Corinth,
and to believers all over Achaia province*

All praise to the God and Father of our Master, Jesus the
Messiah! Father of all mercy! God of all healing counsel! He
comes alongside us when we go through hard times, and
before you know it, he brings us alongside someone else
who is going through hard times so that we can be there for
that person just as God was there for us. We have plenty of

hard times that come from following the Messiah, but no more so than the good times of his healing comfort — we get a full measure of that, too.

2 Corinthians 6:1-10, *from Paul and Timothy to God's congregation in Corinth, and to believers all over Achaia province*

Companions as we are in this work with you, we beg you, please don't squander one bit of this marvelous life God has given us. God reminds us,

I heard your call in the nick of time;
The day you needed me, I was there to help.

Well, now is the right time to listen, the day to be helped. Don't put it off; don't frustrate God's work by showing up late, throwing a question mark over everything we're doing. Our work as God's servants gets validated — or not — in the details. People are watching us as we stay at our post, alertly, unswervingly . . . in hard times, tough times, bad times; when we're beaten up, jailed, and mobbed; working hard, working late, working without eating; with pure heart, clear head, steady hand; in gentleness, holiness, and honest love; when we're telling the truth, and when God's showing his power; when we're doing our best setting things right; when we're praised, and when we're blamed; slandered, and honored; true to our word, though distrusted; ignored by the world, but recognized by God; terrifically alive, though rumored to be dead; beaten within an inch of our lives, but refusing to die; immersed in tears, yet always filled with deep joy; living on handouts, yet enriching many; having nothing, having it all.

2 Thessalonians 3:5, *from Paul, together with Silas and Timothy, to the church of the Thessalonian Christians*

May the Master take you by the hand and lead you along the path of God's love and Christ's endurance.

Hibiscus syriacus flore variegato.
Die syrische Rosenstrauch mit scheckiger Blüthe.

May all the gifts and benefits

that come from God our Father and the

Master, Jesus Christ, be yours!

— 2 CORINTHIANS 1:2

BLESSINGS *for* PROVISION *and* WELL-BEING

Genesis 24:60, *from Rebekah's family to Rebekah*

> You're our sister — live bountifully!
> And your children, triumphantly!

Genesis 27:28-29, *from Isaac to his son, Jacob*

> May God give you
>   of Heaven's dew
>   and Earth's bounty of grain and wine.
> May peoples serve you
>   and nations honor you. . . .
> Those who curse you will be cursed,
>   those who bless you will be blessed.

Genesis 43:14, *from Israel (Jacob) to his sons as his sons prepare to leave for Egypt*

"The Strong God give you grace in that man's eyes. . . ."

Deuteronomy 7:11-15, *from Moses to Israel*

So keep the command and the rules and regulations that I command you today. Do them.

And this is what will happen: When you, on your part, will obey these directives, keeping and following them, GOD, on his part, will keep the covenant of loyal love that he made with your ancestors:

He will love you,
he will bless you,
he will increase you.

He will bless the babies from your womb and the harvest of grain, new wine, and oil from your fields; he'll bless the calves from your herds and lambs from your flocks in the country he promised your ancestors that he'd give you. You'll be blessed beyond all other peoples: no sterility or barrenness in you or your animals. GOD will get rid of all sickness.

Deuteronomy 33:11, *from Moses to the tribe of Levi*

"GOD bless his commitment,
>   stamp your seal of approval on what he does;
Disable the loins of those who defy him,
>   make sure we've heard the last from those who
>   hate him."

Deuteronomy 33:13-16, *from Moses to the tribe of Levi*

"Blessed by GOD be his land:
>   The best fresh dew from high heaven,
>   and fountains springing from the depths;
The best radiance streaming from the sun
>   and the best the moon has to offer;
Beauty pouring off the tops of the mountains
>   and the best from the everlasting hills;
The best of Earth's exuberant gifts,
>   the smile of the Burning-Bush Dweller."

1 Samuel 1:17, *from Eli to Hannah*

"Go in peace. And may the God of Israel give you what you
have asked of him."

2 Samuel 2:6, *from David to the men of Jabesh Gilead*

> "GOD honor you and be true to you — and I'll do the same, matching your generous act of goodness."

2 Samuel 7:28-29, *from David to God*

> "And now, Master GOD, being the God you are, speaking sure words as you do, and having just said this wonderful thing to me, please, just one more thing: Bless my family; keep your eye on them always. You've already as much as said that you would, Master GOD! Oh, may your blessing be on my family permanently!"

1 Chronicles 4:10, *Jabez's request to God*

> "Bless me, O bless me! Give me land, large tracts of land. And provide your personal protection — don't let evil hurt me."

2 Corinthians 1:2, *from Paul and Timothy to God's congregation in Corinth, and to believers all over Achaia province*

> May all the gifts and benefits that come from God our Father and the Master, Jesus Christ, be yours!

2 Corinthians 9:10-11, *from Paul and Timothy to God's congregation in Corinth, and to believers all over Achaia province*

> This most generous God who gives seed to the farmer that becomes bread for your meals is more than extravagant with you. He gives you something you can then give away, which grows into full-formed lives, robust in God, wealthy in every way, so that you can be generous in every way, producing with us great praise to God.

Philippians 4:19-20, *from Paul and Timothy to all the Christians at Philippi*

> You can be sure that God will take care of everything you need, his generosity exceeding even yours in the glory that pours from Jesus. Our God and Father abounds in glory that just pours out into eternity. Yes.

Colossians 1:2, *from Paul, together with Timothy, to the Colossians*

> May everything good from God our Father be yours!

1 Thessalonians 5:23-24, *from Paul, together with Silas and Timothy, to the church at Thessalonica*

> May God himself, the God who makes everything holy and whole, make you holy and whole, put you together — spirit, soul, and body — and keep you fit for the coming of our Master, Jesus Christ. The One who called you is completely dependable. If he said it, he'll do it!

2 Thessalonians 1:2, *from Paul, together with Silas and Timothy, to the church of the Thessalonian Christians*

> Our God gives you everything you need, makes you everything you're to be.

2 Thessalonians 2:16-17, *from Paul, together with Silas and Timothy, to the church of the Thessalonian Christians*

> May Jesus himself and God our Father, who reached out in love and surprised you with gifts of unending help and confidence, put a fresh heart in you, invigorate your work, enliven your speech.

1 Timothy 1:2, *from Paul to Timothy*

> All the best from our God and Christ be yours!

Philemon 25, *from Paul, with his brother Timothy, to Philemon*

> All the best to you from the Master, Jesus Christ!

3 John 2, *from John to his good friend Gaius*

> We're the best of friends, and I pray for good fortune in everything you do, and for your good health — that your everyday affairs prosper, as well as your soul!

Don't panic. I'm with you.

There's no need to fear for I'm your God.

—ISAIAH 41:10

BLESSINGS *of* PROTECTION

Numbers 10:35, *from Moses to God*

> Get up, GOD!
> Put down your enemies!
> Chase those who hate you to the hills!

Judges 5:31, *from Deborah and Barak son of Abinoam*

> May all GOD's enemies perish,
> while his lovers be like the unclouded sun.

Ruth 2:12, *from Boaz to Ruth*

> "GOD reward you well for what you've done — and with a
> generous bonus besides from GOD, to whom you've come
> seeking protection under his wings."

Psalm 28:8-9

> GOD is all strength for his people,
>> ample refuge for his chosen leader;
> Save your people
>> and bless your heritage.
> Care for them;
>> carry them like a good shepherd.

Isaiah 41:10, *from God to his people, Israel*

> Don't panic. I'm with you.
>> There's no need to fear for I'm your God.
> I'll give you strength. I'll help you.
>> I'll hold you steady, keep a firm grip on you.

GOD is all strength for his people,

ample refuge for his chosen leader;

Save your people

and bless your heritage.

Care for them;

carry them like a good shepherd.

— PSALM 28:8-9

GOD's blessing makes life rich;

nothing we do can improve on God.

— Proverbs 10:22

BLESSINGS *for* SEASONS *of* LIFE

Genesis 1:28, *from God to the human beings he created*

> "Prosper! Reproduce! Fill Earth! Take charge!
>   Be responsible for fish in the sea and birds in the air,
>   for every living thing that moves on the face of Earth."

Genesis 28:3-4, *from Isaac to his son Jacob*

> "And may The Strong God bless you and give you many,
> many children, a congregation of peoples; and pass on the
> blessing of Abraham to you and your descendants."

Genesis 48:15-16, *from Israel (Jacob), to Joseph's sons, Ephraim and Manasseh*

> The God before whom walked
>   my fathers Abraham and Isaac,

The God who has been my shepherd
    all my lifelong to this very day,
The Angel who delivered me from every evil,
    Bless the boys.
May my name be echoed in their lives,
    and the names of Abraham and Isaac, my fathers,
And may they grow
    covering the Earth with their children.

Genesis 49:25-26, *from Jacob to his son Joseph*

The God of your father — may he help you!
    And may The Strong God — may he give you his blessings,
Blessings tumbling out of the skies,
    blessings bursting up from the Earth —
    blessings of breasts and womb.
May the blessings of your father
    exceed the blessings of the ancient mountains,
    surpass the delights of the eternal hills.

Ruth 2:19, *from Naomi to Ruth*

"GOD bless whoever it was who took such good care of you!"

Ruth 4:11-12, *from the people in the town square of Bethlehem to Boaz, concerning Ruth*

> "Yes, we are witnesses. May GOD make this woman who is coming into your household like Rachel and Leah, the two women who built the family of Israel. May GOD make you a pillar in Ephrathah and famous in Bethlehem! With the children GOD gives you from this young woman, may your family rival the family of Perez, the son Tamar bore to Judah."

Ruth 4:14, *from the town women of Bethlehem to Naomi*

> "Blessed be GOD! He didn't leave you without family to carry on your life. May this baby grow up to be famous in Israel!"

Psalm 45:1-17, *a wedding song for the sons of Korah*

> My heart bursts its banks,
>   spilling beauty and goodness.
> I pour it out in a poem to the king,
>   shaping the river into words:

"You're the handsomest of men;
    every word from your lips is sheer grace,
    and God has blessed you, blessed you so much.
Strap your sword to your side, warrior!
    Accept praise! Accept due honor!
    Ride majestically! Ride triumphantly!
Ride on the side of truth!
    Ride for the righteous meek!

"Your instructions are glow-in-the-dark;
    you shoot sharp arrows
Into enemy hearts; the king's
    foes lie down in the dust, beaten.

"Your throne is God's throne,
    ever and always;
The scepter of your royal rule
    measures right living.
You love the right
    and hate the wrong.
And that is why God, your very own God,
    poured fragrant oil on your head,
Marking you out as king
    from among your dear companions.

"Your ozone-drenched garments
     are fragrant with mountain breeze.
Chamber music — from the throne room —
     makes you want to dance.
Kings' daughters are maids in your court,
     the Bride glittering with golden jewelry.

"Now listen, daughter, don't miss a word:
     forget your country, put your home behind you.
Be *here* — the king is wild for you.
     Since he's your lord, adore him.
Wedding gifts pour in from Tyre;
     rich guests shower you with presents."

(Her wedding dress is dazzling,
     lined with gold by the weavers;
All her dresses and robes
     are woven with gold.
She is led to the king,
     followed by her virgin companions.
A procession of joy and laughter!
     a grand entrance to the king's palace!)

"Set your mind now on sons —
    don't dote on father and grandfather.
You'll set your sons up as princes
    all over the earth.
I'll make you famous for generations;
    you'll be the talk of the town
    for a long, long time."

Psalm 115:12-15

O GOD, remember us and bless us,
    bless the families of Israel and Aaron.
And let GOD bless all who fear GOD —
    bless the small, bless the great.
Oh, let GOD enlarge your families —
    giving growth to you, growth to your children.
May you be blessed by GOD,
    by GOD, who made heaven and earth.

Psalm 127:5-6

Oh, how blessed are you parents,
    with your quivers full of children!

Your enemies don't stand a chance against you;
    you'll sweep them right off your doorstep.

Psalm 144:12-15

Make our sons in their prime
    like sturdy oak trees,
Our daughters as shapely and bright
    as fields of wildflowers.
Fill our barns with great harvest,
    fill our fields with huge flocks;
Protect us from invasion and exile —
    eliminate the crime in our streets.

How blessed the people who have all this!
How blessed the people who have GOD for God!

Proverbs 5:18-19

Bless your fresh-flowing fountain!
    Enjoy the wife you married as a young man!
Lovely as an angel, beautiful as a rose —
    don't ever quit taking delight in her body.
    Never take her love for granted!

Proverbs 10:22

> GOD's blessing makes life rich;
>> nothing we do can improve on God.

1 Thessalonians 3:10-11, *from Paul, together with Silas and Timothy, to the church at Thessalonica*

> We do what we can, praying away, night and day, asking for the bonus of seeing your faces again and doing what we can to help when your faith falters.
> May God our Father himself and our Master Jesus clear the road to you!

The God of your father — may he help you!

And my the Strong God — may he give you blessings.

GENESIS 49:25

Oh, let GOD enlarge your families –

giving growth to you, growth to your children.

— PSALM 115:14

Blessings *of* Celebration

Psalm 20:5

> When you win, we plan to raise the roof
>> and lead the parade with our banners.
> May all your wishes come true!

Psalm 89:15

> Blessed are the people who know the passwords of praise,
>> who shout on parade in the bright presence of God.

Psalm 118:24

> This is the very day God acted —
>> let's celebrate and be festive!

2 Corinthians 13:9, *from Paul and Timothy to God's congregation in Corinth, and to believers all over Achaia province*

> We don't just put up with our limitations; we celebrate them, and then go on to celebrate every strength, every triumph of the truth in you. We pray hard that it will all come together in your lives.

Blessed are the people who know the passwords of praise,

who shout on parade in the bright presence of GOD.

— PSALM 89:15

I bless you every time I take a breath:

My arms wave like banners of praise to you.

— PSALM 63:4

BLESSINGS *for* GOD

Genesis 14:20, *from Melchizedek, King of Salem, to God*

> And blessed be The High God,
>> who handed your enemies over to you [Abram].

Judges 5:9, *from Deborah and Barak, son of Abinoam, to Israel*

> Lift your hearts high, O Israel,
>> with abandon, volunteering yourselves with the
>> people — bless GOD!

2 Samuel 22:47, *from David to God*

> Live, GOD! Blessing to my Rock,
>> my towering Salvation-God!

1 Kings 8:56-60, *from Solomon to the congregation of Israel*

> "Blessed be GOD, who has given peace to his people Israel
> just as he said he'd do. Not one of all those good and wonder-
> ful words that he spoke through Moses has misfired. May
> GOD, our very own God, continue to be with us just as he was
> with our ancestors — may he never give up and walk out on
> us. May he keep us centered and devoted to him, following
> the life path he has cleared, watching the signposts, walking at
> the pace and rhythms he laid down for our ancestors.
>
> "And let these words that I've prayed in the presence of
> GOD be always right there before him, day and night, so that
> he'll do what is right for me, to guarantee justice for his
> people Israel day after day after day. Then all the people on
> earth will know GOD is the true God; there is no other God.
> And *you*, your lives must be totally obedient to GOD, our
> personal God, following the life path he has cleared, alert
> and attentive to everything he has made plain this day."

1 Chronicles 16:36, *from the people of Israel to God*

> Blessed be GOD, the God of Israel,
> from everlasting to everlasting.

1 Chronicles 29:10-13, *from David to God*

> Blessed are you, GOD of Israel, our father
>> from of old and forever.
> To you, O GOD, belong the greatness and the might,
>> the glory, the victory, the majesty, the splendor;
> Yes! Everything in heaven, everything on earth;
>> the kingdom all yours! You've raised yourself high over all.
> Riches and glory come from you,
>> you're ruler over all;
> You hold strength and power in the palm of your hand
>> to build up and strengthen all.
> And here we are, O God our God, giving thanks to you,
>> praising your splendid Name.

1 Chronicles 29:20, *from David to the congregation of the leaders of Israel*

> Bless GOD, your God!

Nehemiah 9:5-6, *from the people of Israel to God*

> Blessed be your glorious name,
>> exalted above all blessing and praise!

You're the one,
> GOD, you alone;
You made the heavens,
> the heavens of heavens, and all angels;
The earth and everything on it,
> the seas and everything in them;
You keep them all alive;
> heaven's angels worship you!

Psalm 18:46

> Live, GOD! Blessings from my Rock,
> > my free and freeing God, towering!

Psalm 26:12

> I'm on the level with you, GOD;
> > I bless you every chance I get.

Psalm 28:6-7, *from David to God*

> Blessed be GOD —
> > he heard me praying.
> He proved he's on my side;
> > I've thrown my lot in with him.

Now I'm jumping for joy,
>> and shouting and singing my thanks to him.

Psalm 31:21, *from David to God*

Blessed GOD!
>> His love is the wonder of the world.

Psalm 34:1, *from David to God*

I bless GOD every chance I get;
my lungs expand with his praise.

Psalm 40:4-5, *from David*

Blessed are you who give yourselves over to GOD,
>> turn your backs on the world's "sure thing,"
>> ignore what the world worships;
The world's a huge stockpile
>> of GOD-wonders and God-thoughts.
Nothing and no one
>> comes close to you!
I start talking about you, telling what I know,
>> and quickly run out of words.

Neither numbers nor words
account for you.

Psalm 41:13, *from David to God*

Blessed is GOD, Israel's God,
always, always, always.
Yes. Yes. Yes.

Psalm 63:4

I bless you every time I take a breath;
My arms wave like banners of praise to you.

Psalm 66:8-12

Bless our God, O peoples!
Give him a thunderous welcome!
Didn't he set us on the road to life?
Didn't he keep us out of the ditch?
He trained us first,
passed us like silver through refining fires,
Brought us into hardscrabble country,
pushed us to our very limit,

Road-tested us inside and out,
> took us to hell and back;
Finally he brought us
> to this well-watered place.

Psalm 66:16-20

All believers, come here and listen,
> let me tell you what God did for me.
I called out to him with my mouth,
> my tongue shaped the sounds of music.
If I had been cozy with evil,
> the Lord would never have listened.
But he most surely *did* listen,
> he came on the double when he heard my prayer.
Blessed be God: he didn't turn a deaf ear,
> he stayed with me, loyal in his love.

Psalm 67

God, mark us with grace
> and blessing! Smile!
The whole country will see how you work,
> all the godless nations see how you save.

God! Let people thank and enjoy you.
  Let all people thank and enjoy you.
Let all far-flung people become happy
  and shout their happiness because
You judge them fair and square,
  you tend the far-flung peoples.
God! Let people thank and enjoy you.
  Let all people thank and enjoy you.
Earth, display your exuberance!
  You mark us with blessing, O God, our God.
You mark us with blessing, O God.
  Earth's four corners — honor him!

Psalm 68:19-20, *from David to God*

Blessed be the Lord —
  day after day he carries us along.
He's our Savior, our God, oh yes!
  He's God-for-us, he's God-who-saves-us.

Psalm 68:26

The whole choir blesses God.
  Like a fountain of praise, Israel blesses GOD.

Psalm 68:35

> A terrible beauty, O God,
>> streams from your sanctuary.
> It's Israel's strong God! He gives
>> power and might to his people!
> O you, his people — bless God!

Psalm 72:18-20, *from King Solomon to God*

> Blessed GOD, Israel's God,
>> the one and only wonder-working God!
> Blessed always his blazing glory!
>> All earth brims with his glory.
> Yes and Yes and Yes.

Psalm 80:19

> GOD, God of the angel armies, come back!
> Smile your blessing smile:
> *That* will be our salvation.

Psalm 89:51, *from Ethan to God*

> Blessed be GOD forever and always!
>> Yes. Oh, yes.

Psalm 103, *from David to God*

> O my soul, bless GOD.
>> From head to toe, I'll bless his holy name!
> O my soul, bless GOD,
>> don't forget a single blessing!
>
>> He forgives your sins — every one.
>> He heals your diseases — every one.
>> He redeems you from hell — saves your life!
>> He crowns you with love and mercy — a paradise crown.
>> He wraps you in goodness — beauty eternal.
>> He renews your youth — you're always young in his
> presence.
>
> GOD makes everything come out right;
>> he puts victims back on their feet.
> He showed Moses how he went about his work,
>> opened up his plans to all Israel.
> GOD is sheer mercy and grace;
>> not easily angered, he's rich in love.
> He doesn't endlessly nag and scold,
>> nor hold grudges forever.
> He doesn't treat us as our sins deserve,
>> nor pay us back in full for our wrongs.

As high as heaven is over the earth,

    so strong is his love to those who fear him.

And as far as sunrise is from sunset,

    he has separated us from our sins.

As parents feel for their children,

    GOD feels for those who fear him.

He knows us inside and out,

    keeps in mind that we're made of mud.

Men and women don't live very long;

    like wildflowers they spring up and blossom,

But a storm snuffs them out just as quickly,

    leaving nothing to show they were here.

GOD's love, though, is ever and always,

    eternally present to all who fear him,

Making everything right for them and their children

    as they follow his Covenant ways

    and remember to do whatever he said.

GOD has set his throne in heaven;

    he rules over us all. He's the King!

So bless GOD, you angels,

    ready and able to fly at his bidding,

    quick to hear and do what he says.

Bless GOD, all you armies of angels,
>   alert to respond to whatever he wills.
Bless GOD, all creatures, wherever you are —
>   everything and everyone made by GOD.

And you, O my soul, bless GOD!

Psalm 104

>   O my soul, bless GOD!

GOD, my God, how great you are!
>   beautifully, gloriously robed,
Dressed up in sunshine,
>   and all heaven stretched out for your tent.
You built your palace on the ocean deeps,
>   made a chariot out of clouds and took off on wind-wings.
You commandeered winds as messengers,
>   appointed fire and flame as ambassadors.
You set earth on a firm foundation
>   so that nothing can shake it, ever.
You blanketed earth with ocean,
>   covered the mountains with deep waters;
Then you roared and the water ran away —
>   your thunder crash put it to flight.

Mountains pushed up, valleys spread out
  in the places you assigned them.
You set boundaries between earth and sea;
  never again will earth be flooded.
You started the springs and rivers,
  sent them flowing among the hills.
All the wild animals now drink their fill,
  wild donkeys quench their thirst.
Along the riverbanks the birds build nests,
  ravens make their voices heard.
You water the mountains from your heavenly cisterns;
  earth is supplied with plenty of water.
You make grass grow for the livestock,
  hay for the animals that plow the ground.

Oh yes, God brings grain from the land,
  wine to make people happy,
Their faces glowing with health,
  a people well-fed and hearty.
GOD's trees are well-watered —
  the Lebanon cedars he planted.
Birds build their nests in those trees;
  look — the stork at home in the treetop.

Mountain goats climb about the cliffs;
> badgers burrow among the rocks.
The moon keeps track of the seasons,
> the sun is in charge of each day.
When it's dark and night takes over,
> all the forest creatures come out.
The young lions roar for their prey,
> clamoring to God for their supper.
When the sun comes up, they vanish,
> lazily stretched out in their dens.
Meanwhile, men and women go out to work,
> busy at their jobs until evening.

What a wildly wonderful world, GOD!
> You made it all, with Wisdom at your side,
> made earth overflow with your wonderful creations.
Oh, look — the deep, wide sea,
> brimming with fish past counting,
> sardines and sharks and salmon.
Ships plow those waters,
> and Leviathan, your pet dragon, romps in them.
All the creatures look expectantly to you
> to give them their meals on time.

You come, and they gather around;
        you open your hand and they eat from it.
If you turned your back,
        they'd die in a minute —
Take back your Spirit and they die,
        revert to original mud;
Send out your Spirit and they spring to life —
        the whole countryside in bloom and blossom.

The glory of GOD — let it last forever!
        Let GOD enjoy his creation!
He takes one look at earth and triggers an earthquake,
        points a finger at the mountains, and volcanoes erupt.

Oh, let me sing to GOD all my life long,
        sing hymns to my God as long as I live!
Oh, let my song please him;
        I'm so pleased to be singing to GOD.
But clear the ground of sinners —
        no more godless men and women!

Oh my soul, bless GOD!

Psalm 106:48

> Blessed be GOD, Israel's God!
> Bless now, bless always!
> Oh! Let everyone say Amen!
> Hallelujah!

Psalm 119:12-16

> Be blessed, GOD;
> train me in your ways of wise living.
> I'll transfer to my lips
> all the counsel that comes from your mouth;
> I delight far more in what you tell me about living
> than in gathering a pile of riches.
> I ponder every morsel of wisdom from you,
> I attentively watch how you've done it.
> I relish everything you've told me of life,
> I won't forget a word of it.

Psalm 124:6-8, *from David to God*

> Oh, blessed be GOD!
> He didn't go off and leave us.

He didn't abandon us defenseless,
> helpless as a rabbit in a pack of snarling dogs.

We've flown free from their fangs,
> free of their traps, free as a bird.

Their grip is broken;
> we're free as a bird in flight.

GOD's strong name is our help,
> the same GOD who made heaven and earth.

Psalm 134, *A pilgrim song*

Come, bless GOD,
> all you servants of GOD!

You priests of GOD, posted to the nightwatch
> in GOD's shrine,

Lift your praising hands to the Holy Place,
> and bless GOD.

In turn, may GOD of Zion bless you —
> GOD who made heaven and earth!

Psalm 135:21

> Oh, blessed be GOD of Zion,
>> First Citizen of Jerusalem!
> Hallelujah!

Psalm 144:1, *from David to God*

> Blessed be GOD, my mountain,
>> who trains me to fight fair and well.

Psalm 145, *from David to God*

> I lift you high in praise, my God, O my King!
>> and I'll bless your name into eternity.

> I'll bless you every day,
>> and keep it up from now to eternity.

> GOD is magnificent; he can never be praised enough.
>> There are no boundaries to his greatness.

> Generation after generation stands in awe of your work;
>> each one tells stories of your mighty acts.

> Your beauty and splendor have everyone talking;
>> I compose songs on your wonders.

Your marvelous doings are headline news;
 I could write a book full of the details of your greatness.

The fame of your goodness spreads across the country;
 your righteousness is on everyone's lips.

GOD is all mercy and grace —
 not quick to anger, is rich in love.

GOD is good to one and all;
 everything he does is suffused with grace.

Creation and creatures applaud you, GOD;
 your holy people bless you.

They talk about the glories of your rule,
 they exclaim over your splendor,

Letting the world know of your power for good,
 the lavish splendor of your kingdom.

Your kingdom is a kingdom eternal;
 you never get voted out of office.

GOD always does what he says,
 and is gracious in everything he does.

GOD gives a hand to those down on their luck,
    gives a fresh start to those ready to quit.

All eyes are on you, expectant;
    you give them their meals on time.

Generous to a fault,
    you lavish your favor on all creatures.

Everything GOD does is right —
    the trademark on all his works is love.

GOD's there, listening for all who pray,
    for all who pray and mean it.

He does what's best for those who fear him —
    hears them call out, and saves them.

GOD sticks by all who love him,
    but it's all over for those who don't.

My mouth is filled with GOD's praise.
    Let everything living bless him,
    bless his holy name from now to eternity!

Ezekiel 3:12

"Blessed be the Glory of GOD in his Sanctuary!"

Daniel 2:20-23, *from Daniel to God*

"Blessed be the name of God,
    forever and ever.
He knows all, does all:
    He changes the seasons and guides history,
He raises up kings and also brings them down,
    he provides both intelligence and discernment,
He opens up the depths, tells secrets,
    sees in the dark — light spills out of him!
God of all my ancestors, all thanks! all praise!

Mark 11:9-10, *from the people to Jesus*

Hosanna!
Blessed is he who comes in God's name!
Blessed the coming kingdom of our father David!
Hosanna in highest heaven!

Luke 1:68, *from Zachariah*

> Blessed be the Lord, the God of Israel;
>> he came and set his people free.

Luke 19:38, *from the crowd of disciples to Jesus*

> Blessed is he who comes,
>> the king in God's name!
> All's well in heaven!
>> Glory in the high places!

Romans 16:25-27, *from Paul to all of the Christians in Rome*

All of our praise rises to the One who is strong enough to make *you* strong, exactly as preached in Jesus Christ, precisely as revealed in the mystery kept secret for so long but now an open book through the prophetic Scriptures. All the nations of the world can now know the truth and be brought into obedient belief, carrying out the orders of God, who got all this started, down to the very last letter.

All our praise is focused through Jesus on this incomparably wise God! Yes!

Ephesians 1:3-10, *from Paul to the faithful Christians in Ephesus*

How blessed is God! And what a blessing he is! He's the
Father of our Master, Jesus Christ, and takes us to the high
places of blessing in him. Long before he laid down earth's
foundations, he had us in mind, had settled on us as the
focus of his love, to be made whole and holy by his love.
Long, long ago he decided to adopt us into his family
through Jesus Christ. (What pleasure he took in planning
this!) He wanted us to enter into the celebration of his lavish
gift-giving by the hand of his beloved Son.

Because of the sacrifice of the Messiah, his blood poured
out on the altar of the Cross, we're a free people — free of
penalties and punishments chalked up by all our misdeeds.
And not just barely free, either. *Abundantly* free! He thought of
everything, provided for everything we could possibly need,
letting us in on the plans he took such delight in making. He
set it all out before us in Christ, a long-range plan in which
everything would be brought together and summed up in him,
everything in deepest heaven, everything on planet earth.

Ephesians 3:20-21, *from Paul to the faithful Christians in Ephesus*

> God can do anything, you know — far more than you could ever imagine or guess or request in your wildest dreams! He does it not by pushing us around but by working within us, his Spirit deeply and gently within us.
>
> Glory to God in the church!
> Glory to God in the Messiah, in Jesus!
> Glory down all the generations!
> Glory through all millennia! Oh, yes!